While every precaution has been taken i
the publisher assumes no responsibility
damages resulting from the use of the ir

UNAPOLOGETIC BLUE BUTTERFLY (POEMS FOR HEALING)

First edition. June 10, 2024.

Copyright © 2024 CeeCee The Butterfly.

ISBN: 979-8227277060

Written by CeeCee The Butterfly.

[Unapologetic Blue Butterfly (Poems For Healing)]

Melanin Kissed Skin 14
The Healing Process!!! 15
Losing Me 16
Tearstained Pillowcases 17
Spiraling 18
Inner Beauty 19
Triggers 20
A Person Lost 21
Just Being Me! 22
Scattered Dreams 23
Internal Happiness 24
Safe Place 25
Cold Hearted 26
Yearning For Love 27
Enough 28
Growth 29
Forever Evolving 30
Dear Little Me 31
Healing From My Trauma 32

beautiful blue butterfly

In life we go through changes and we all start out as an egg, later down the line we grow into a larva. In order to grow we had to eat and to eat was to survive. Once we ate and had all we could store we went into a deep slumber in our cocoon. To hibernate, to grow, to gain our wings, but see right before the cocoon is made that the larva is a caterpillar that's eager to find its place in the world alongside the other winged animals.

A caterpillar spends months preparing for the day that it will be able to make its cocoon and gain its wings. But for one special butterfly the beautiful blue one that tugs at my heart. I learned this beautiful blue butterfly never could gain her wings because she was afraid and no one around her seemed to care. She spent all her days and months not being able to eat because depression had decided to move in permanently without warning her first.

Maybe just maybe the beautiful blue caterpillar will indeed become the beautiful blue butterfly she's longing to be but she has to trust the road she's on will produce the fruit she wants it to bear as she awaits her turn, her cocoon finally begins to form and before she knows it she is on her way to gain those beautiful blue wings. She waiting to fly away.

In her cocoon she waits and dreams of the day she'll be free to spread her beautiful blue wings as she soars through the sky for the whole world to get a glimpse of how beautiful things are when we wait for them to grow. Out of her cocoon she soars, fluttering through the summer air in hopes to find her true self and maybe even true love.

This beautiful blue butterfly now needs to gain some confidence in herself that she is growing, glowing and will eventually have her time to shine. She's scared, timid ,worried that everything will go wrong. She's losing herself as she fights for those that she loves. Lost and confused racing thoughts, thoughts of clipping of her beautiful blue wings to fly no longer. This beautiful blue butterfly has to remain strong so out in the world as they knock her down she refuses to stay defeated.

This beautiful blue butterfly has gained the courage to live , to love, laugh and just be her beautiful strong self. Without the self doubt, self defeating acts and suicidal thoughts she fight against everything that was placed in her way to take her out but she refuses to go down to without putting up a fight. She is unique, strong, determined, self confident, and it all shows within her beautifully constructed blue wings.

She is a beautiful blue butterfly at last!

Mind On Overload

Lately, yes lately
My mind has been in
What would seem to be
Complete overdrive
Constantly spinning
Never ceasing to think
Of things I could or
Should have done
BETTER!

To say it's in high speed
Could very well down play
The complete severity
Of how deep in overload it is
Always awaiting approval from
Those same people who could
Truly give a fuck less
If it lives or dies but yet
It still seeks the full validation.

My mind fully loaded with the tools
It needs to survive but bending,
Folding, even breaking with every
Tear, every hurt , every memory
That shields the traumatizing and
Detrimental truth of each past hurt,
Relationship, situation, circumstance

This beautiful blue butterfly now needs to gain some confidence in herself that she is growing, glowing and will eventually have her time to shine. She's scared, timid ,worried that everything will go wrong. She's losing herself as she fights for those that she loves. Lost and confused racing thoughts, thoughts of clipping of her beautiful blue wings to fly no longer. This beautiful blue butterfly has to remain strong so out in the world as they knock her down she refuses to stay defeated.

This beautiful blue butterfly has gained the courage to live , to love, laugh and just be her beautiful strong self. Without the self doubt, self defeating acts and suicidal thoughts she fight against everything that was placed in her way to take her out but she refuses to go down to without putting up a fight. She is unique, strong, determined, self confident, and it all shows within her beautifully constructed blue wings.

She is a beautiful blue butterfly at last!

Mind On Overload

Lately, yes lately
My mind has been in
What would seem to be
Complete overdrive
Constantly spinning
Never ceasing to think
Of things I could or
Should have done
BETTER!

To say it's in high speed
Could very well down play
The complete severity
Of how deep in overload it is
Always awaiting approval from
Those same people who could
Truly give a fuck less
If it lives or dies but yet
It still seeks the full validation.

My mind fully loaded with the tools
It needs to survive but bending,
Folding, even breaking with every
Tear, every hurt , every memory
That shields the traumatizing and
Detrimental truth of each past hurt,
Relationship, situation, circumstance

That life has thrown in its path
To put a stop to its journey.

See my mind is always in overload
Because it holds the truth of my past
That I can't even begin to share with
Others because it's become so
Accustom to caring what others
May say , do or think!
But see what I learned is those same
Thoughts , words and even actions
Come from those same people who
Could give a damn less
If my mind and I live or die!

But today I care out loud
Not in fear of those people but
In gear that my life could very well
Be on it's very last breath
Cause see I want to die and yes
I have tried to commit suicide
As I hide from the pain with this
Plastered on smile dying inside
Cause if the things that I have
Seen , heard and been through in
My little life continue to replay
Over and over in my head.

Cause my mind to go into

High speed overdrive
Cause me to rip at the seams
Desperately fighting against
Depression , suicidal thoughts,
anxiety, worthlessness, anger, sadness and
So much more that no matter how hard I try
nothing seems to get better and no one
Even gives a fuck about my wellbeing
As I scream and cry out for help
Risking being placed under a psychiatric
Hold because that would cause me to lose
The only thing keeping me together.

But even with everything I go through
My daughter keeps me pushing through
Through the overload and overcrowded
Headspace that's always fighting for validation
and love and always seeming
To fall short but also to the girl that
Seemingly gave up on herself and
Her hopes and dreams to make
A difference that everyone can see
Because each day she's losing herself
And no longer can she fight of the
Breathtaking amount of pain.

Suicidal thought creep back up
And she try's not to write that letter to
The one person who keeps her sane
Because that person can't read yet and

that person needs her the most
But she doesn't want to continue the
Fight with a mind that won't even
Running so fast that all she can do is
Cry.

Cause my minds in overload!!!!!

Rock Bottom

So many times I've heard so many people talk about how they've hit rock bottom but can never describe what rock bottom truly feels like. See for me I can truly say I've hit rock bottom but I refuse to stay there.

See I've been through so much in a short period of time that to go over even the past years events you would feel as though your thoughts of hitting rock bottom are invalid but see everyone faces a different type of rock bottom but not many choose to get up and fight.

In the past year I've lost friends and family who promised to always be there, I've buried the only other grandmother who took the time to get to know me and make that connection, I've been homeless, jobless, depressed, anxious, suicidal at times, irritable, lonely and so many others.

At first I said man I should just give up nothing is going right and it won't get any better till I truly hit my rock bottom. I admitted myself into the psychiatric ward at a local hospital and the doctors had me stay there over night with no means of communication with the outside world.

While I was there I learn the true definition of hitting rock bottom but also the true definition of a fighter and a survivor. See I finally realized my value and worth after being mistreated , abused, lied on , cheated on, having to fight for my daughter, to never being in one place for more the two months at a time.

I was properly diagnosed with everything I had told the doctors I had for years. I tried to tell the doctor I had symptoms of but they would never listen and now I realized that I remained in that defeated rock bottom state of mind and living for too long that I had to fight even harder to get out of it.

See once you hit rock bottom the only way you can truly go is UP unless you choose to stay down, defeated and not willing to fight. Me I couldn't possible do that because I valued myself and my worth but mostly because of my daughter who needs me.

Today I can say if you're willing to fight for you that you too can come up out of that state of being and mind.

FIGHT FOR YOU!!! No one else can do it for you but you

Numb

I was asked the other day why do I seem to be so numb to the world and everything going on in and around it. So I looked at that person and responded just like this I'm numb to the world and everything within and around it because I learned to adapt to things that always bring me pain, sorrow, and hard times.

See my friend I've become so accustomed to this numbing feeling I get that I don't truly realize when I'm upset , when I've cried or most importantly when l last laughed or smiled.

I've grown numb to feelings of progression and regression, to guilt and forgiveness to simply being happy with who I am and everything that I have accomplished and have yet to accomplished.

Use to trying to live up to others standards that I forget to merely live and achieve my own , so I can continue to raise the standard. Believing that nothing I accomplish is worth the praise or even the recognition because society has me believing that I'm less than because I struggle.

Struggle to love myself more than I love others, struggle to get by, struggle make and keep genuine friends close and even struggle just being me flaws and all because you've all tried to reprogram my brain into think like you instead of herself.

Finding answers amongst the self medicating cloud and empty bottles of lush wine that quenches A thirst I was unaware existed till it hit me, learning to push away everyone who could truly care because already damaged goods that nobody will ever love.

Maybe even losing myself repeatedly to feel loved and wanted but not realizing the ones who have truly loved me for me from the day we met. Those ones who loved me more than I even loved myself who pushed me to never give up I thank you.

See cause without those handful of people I wouldn't even still be alive to speak my truth and explore who the real me truly is I thank the most high for never giving up on me for fighting for me when i felt to weak and torn down.

So now when I'm asked why I seems so numb I simply state that I'm not at all numb just fully adapted to this life I live and regaining my footing once again. Because I am indeed a girl in progress!

Drowning

These days I feel like I'm drowning, unable to breathe. Drowning but no one even seems to care to the point where I wish that there was no me but even though I feel like I'm drowning I never let my head fall underneath the waters.

See if not for me I have to stand ten toes down in this crazy cold hearted world for my precious daughter because that is the assignment that I was given so while I feel like I was drowning I never drowned in the endless sea of shame and regret.

To feel like I'm drowning , is a very numbing feeling that I can't even begin to describe. I truly don't trust a soul outta fear that they will let me down again. Losing myself in a world that doesn't give a damn about me or my child regardless of what people may let slip outta their mouths.

If I allow myself to drown I know surely my daughter might pick up the same self-defeating habits which would cause her to drown in her own ways and that I couldn't live with so I struggle to stay afloat even when I would rather submerge all of me into those cold waters to freeze over.

So yes I'm drowning and sometimes longing to give into the suicidal thoughts and all the vivid nightmares that plague me when I lay upon my tearstained pillowcases, fighting to find enough peace to sleep but soon abruptly woken up by dreams of me dying.

They said time would heal those wounds and scars but I say no matter how much time goes by I will never truly forget the pain I endured that left me numb to all the things in the world causing me to feel like I'm drowning although I am still afloat.

Broken

So many days go by that I have to pick up the pieces of myself, the pieces that you promised you wouldn't break again, see my biggest weakness is I love unconditionally and I never stop loving you but in return you never reciprocate the same love.

Dangling from a string is my heart in your hands wishing you could see that I'm truly trying to be the one you need see I have a disposition to loving others more than I can love myself and that's why things always fail.

I call it a disposition because time and time again I wish I could just stop my heart from falling and caring so that I can't protect it from the let downs, the lies and hurt that you will end up causing.

I'm broken into pieces as I express how my heart is starting to become numb to all the pain it has to endure, the pain has impacted my heart in a way that it has a numbing affect to when you live and the love you once said you had for me is gone.

I'm broken and bruised but that only because of the scars and wounds you have afflicted to my heart because that once ever loving me is dying slowly every time she is hurt she's becoming use to getting hurt and mistreated.

Only time will tell what will happen when she truly gives up in love completely not only to give others but most importantly to herself she lost and confused and forever scarred by the lies and the accusations you have stated and how you question her ability to love you the right way.

She lives hard and she loves unconditionally so she stops Day after day from hurting herself when she hesitates to tell you she loves you because once spoken she can't ever take it back. But now she has to learn to love herself more than she loves anyone.

Rebirth

These days I feel like I'm going through a rebirthing, redefining and growth change. Most days I feel lost and in disarray unable to share my true thoughts and feelings. I just want to be free, free from dismay and defeat. Free from the comfortable and known. Free from me

Most days I sit with my head held down in defeat but deeply longing for a connection that will never severe. A connection that will help me to embrace myself once again, see I'm being rebirth and changed.

These days I feel so alone like nobody truly gets me, understands me, values me or needs me. Most days I'm just an endless ball of uncertainty just going through the motions you see. Right now I feel like I'm drowning in all the thoughts of me.

This rebirth is just a transitional stage for me. It's a process that I must endure to recreate, redefine and rebirth the me that I'm destined to be. Everything that I have encountered and endured has been for that reason alone.

Now these days I walk with my head held high and my crown upright not allowing things, places and people to cause me to question who I am at my core. These days I smile brighter than before and it's just so contagious.

No past hurt can change that for me I'm loving this phase of rebirth I'm in and nothing will change that for me. Say hello to the new redefined healed version of me.

The Calm Before The Storm

They said I'm like the calm before the storm, that little glimmer of light out over the raging sea. The thin line between the sky and the sea. That ever so awkward feeling you get that puts you on the edge of your seat

The feeling you get when you're unsure of the outcome or what role you play. The mixed up emotions and Unhealed traumas from the innermost part of yourself, that threatens to resurface from the dark abyss of you mind casting tumultuous waves all in and throughout your life.

See me I'm the calm before the storm, the stillness of a ticking time clock counting down each second , each minute and each hour waiting to release the years of suppressed feelings and emotions, alongside my own traumas and generational traumas and curses.

My calm over the years has evolved, leaving me unsure of the way I might react or if I'll react at all. My calm these days just ain't as calm anymore shit but can you blame me for that. For years, and I do mean years 26 damn years to be exact I've be silenced.

Told to push my feelings down and not express them, taught to stay in a child's place and never tell anyone not even family what goes on in anyone else's house even if it is hurting me. Told that I've always been naive and this is just the way the universe wishes to repay me.

Lost, confused, downright defeated the calm in me has begun to boil up steaming like the vegetables you steam in your cooking pots. Searching and praying for just one person who will just listen and no not listen to solve the problem or to simply have a response. But for someone who would dare to be different and just want to understand.

Tick Tock tick tock goes the timer on my calm because nowadays I am struggling to regain control over my calm before it turns into a storm. This beautiful crafted majestic blue butterfly has reached her limit bursting out the seam of my cocoon do I dare unleash my storm

Manipulated , abused, silenced and damn sure misunderstood I look around and silently respond to my calm, it's time to release the storm that's within me. So I can heal and grow cause God for damn sure knows I've learned and continue to learn what it truly means to be THE CALM BEFORE THE STORM

Bottled Up Emotions

Here are the words I thought I would never speak, the dreams I thought I would never dream.

The words of hurt and fear, of betrayal and tears, the words that from time to time I'm scared to speak.

The words I'm scared to say like I love you and I miss you, because of the fear of being hurt and mistreated all over again.

These are all some of the plethora of emotions that remain bottled up inside of me, and sealed with one of the most convincing smiles you have ever seen.

All these bottled up emotions on the brink of exploding right in front of the world to be seen, heard and judge once again.

To continue the never ending cycle of pretending not to care, not to hurt but deep down inside dying from the hurt, the pain, confusion and betrayal.

All these emotions rapidly spinning within me and all my feelings being displayed for the whole world to see because unfortunately for me, with every emotion I bottle in, I wear it on my sleeves.

My eyes tell my story before my lips even move and for most people they never understand how hard it is to just let go of some hurts, it's constant battle.

But no more will I bottle up my emotions I will speak up, and let those who hurt me and persecute me will no longer be triumphant over me or my mind, I'm taking back control.

No more Bottled Up Emotions! No More!

Battered!, Wounded!, Scarred!

In the making of a warrior
    there will always be so many
    wounds and scars
    every attack leaves you
    a battered soul.
    Being bettered, wounded
    scarred leaves you with a
    story to tell, that no one
    else can write or
    tell it for you because
    only you know the
    TRUTH!
    Battered!, Wounded!, Scarred!
    I can not believe what
    my life has become
    since that night,
    but I vowed never to
    waste anymore of
    my time and life.
    To become a warrior
    you first have to endure
    a world of pain and anger,
    even some heartache and confusion
    but it all leads to you
    being able to fight on
    day by day, one day at a time.
    Battered!, Wounded!, Scarred!
    but never let it determine
    just WHO YOU ARE!

Amongst The Embers

Amongst the embers you found me so lost and afraid, my heart shattered into a million tiny pieces from some pain I can't explain. There I was laying lifeless until you came in piecing me back together shred by shred.

Amongst the embers I fell so confused and alone, not sure if anyone would notice shit can they even tell. My heart is wounded yet I still keep going on giving love to those who couldn't even bother to answer the phone.

Not one call, one text, a simple just checking in I go unnoticed by some of my closest friends. My heart is aching in this endless abyss of feelings and emotions I feel but some how you pulled me up from the embers and I'm whole again.

Falling in love with myself even more as she continues on, no matter what life has thrown her way. She keeps on fighting until she's complete and someone is willing to receive her as she is. Amongst The Embers we sit and realize that the person we need most is always ourselves.

So out from amongst the embers I emerge truer to myself than before. Loving every piece of me for who I truly am not hiding in the embers afraid to shine as bright as I am suppose to because others are afraid of my glow. Out from amongst the embers my heart is complete and whole with this newfound love I have for every aspect that is ME!

Midnight Cries

The tears that fall at night
    Those tears come from deep inside
    So far within that I'm unsure all the time
    But why do those tears continue to fall you ask?
    It's because I'm deeply broken inside
    I toss and I turn from all the thoughts
    That continue to wander aimlessly throughout my mind, the ones that no matter how much you try to turn them off they stay on Throughout the night.
    I call them my midnight cries because
    While everyone else is resting soundly
    In their bed my thoughts begin to spin and twirl throughout my head
    I begin to weep and stir
    I look around and notice that no one every notices how unsoundly I sleep at night.
    Those midnight cries stem from years Of running and years of denial that I tried to hide inside.
    Although I feel like nobody hears my cries I know that god is trying to heal me inside I cautiously toss and turn without disturbing a soul Left up to fear the unknown the thoughts that appear as monsters in my dreams.
    The dreams that turn into continuous nightmares like the one where my daughter goes missing and nobody can find her or even where she dies at the end of each dream. Lord knows to sleep is to be left wondering what if and why ? And never receiving the answers that I continuously look around for.
    See only god knows why he placed me on the path I'm on but all I know is that I fight this thoughts, dreams, nightmares constantly that lead to a face painted from those midnight cries that fall ever so endlessly

even when I pretend that everything is okay. Only those closest to me know that something is wrong.

See me I was always a very happy go lucky kid until I experienced one traumatic thing after another. See those things and feeling go without mentioning because once they're unleashed many unforeseen things can begin to happen. I never truly understood what one meant by someone looking like what they been through and vise versa.

See even if you looked at me you could not even begin to imagine the things I've heard, seen, spoken or even touched because once again I do not look like what I have been through or where I am going but known that my story can touch the hearts of not only the youngest person but the oldest as well.

Hears the beginnings of my midnight cries and why oh why they continue to go unnoticed throughout the night.

Getting Back To Me

Lately it's been so hard for me to find myself again lost in a world where my innocence was taken before my life even truly began. Lost in an infinite loop, feeling like I was drowning in a deep dark abyss of lost dreams and shattered promises. Praying that one day someone would take the time to just understand who I truly am.

See at age three I was being molested by a man who was suppose to protect me from those things and family swear I was lying then, age 18 came around and lord knows hell began for me right then raped and then blamed everyone said I was to naïve back then and damn I should've knew better than.

Better than to talk to a stranger and not think the worst of them but how could I when my trauma had already settled in from what that man did to me way back then, searching for ways to better fill the void then. Thinking I had no value and no purpose to live.

Partying every night being promiscuous, drinking and popping pills I should've knew better than to believe another when he said he could love me better than. Knowing damn well I never really knew what love was then.

Went to sleep every night crying praying for better days, burying family and friends became so regular to me then. One or two every few months then followed up with arms full of scars cause I was cutting just to get back closer to them.

See depression had finally settled in, my self worth seem every fleeting then no sense of direction I sure wasn't seeing clear back then. Made some good friends throughout the years they sure helped me get back to myself.

Had a baby girl and still raising her without a man. Learned that not everyone can go with me when it's time for me to win. Finally picked back up this pen and put it back to the paper but still unsure of how receptive others are gonna be but damn.

I'm starting not to give a damn because they only one I'm really trying to save is me again, with every line I write my heart fills complete again. Not looking for love I'm finally at peace my friend. Me and my daughter got bigger dreams my friends.

See years past and I'm finally realizing that everything that was placed before only helped me grow thicker skin. Helped me to better decipher between what fake and real. I'm finally getting back to me and god knows I'm loving it here.

Finally feeling complete no more numbing feels. Cause I finally found my voice, my peace and stronger than I've ever been. Don't count me out cause I'm destined to win!

Melanin Kissed Skin

Feels like I'm losing myself in your melanin kissed skin, that light bronze honey colored complexion that has a way of drawing me in, driving me crazier and crazier as I look at you with my dark chestnut colored eyes. You have a way of speaking to the innermost parts of me that no one has spoken to before.

With your soft caring tone and your perfectly sculpted arms that you carefully wrap around me I've fallen for your mind more than I have fallen for anything else in this world. You leave me speechless and unafraid, with every embrace I fall even more with every kiss stole I daydream about what this love could possibly be.

As I get lost in your touch as you discover exactly what my love language is, I begin to understand yours as well. While we learn each other we lay and bask in each others aura fallen more in love with one another than we dare to before. See when we meet and I laid my eyes on your skin that is perfectly kissed and glowing with melanin.

It's the way the sun illuminates your skin and the way your skin feels when I rub up against you. Never in a million years did I think I would fall so fast for someone but still have enough willpower to get lost in you but not rushing the outcome. With you I feel whole again and with you I am beginning to realize my worth again.

Your melanin kissed skin has always had a way of making me feel secure and worthy. Maybe even happier than I've ever been in the past and for that I can only fall more in love with how you get to know my mind before even diving in between my thighs to one of the most sacred places on my body.

See with you it's not about sex or a quick nut, but instead with you it's about healing and restoring. You focus on getting to know me and providing me with the intimacy I didn't even realize I was longing for which draws me in even more. My ability to be open with you is a test but with everything moment we share becomes easier to do.

At first I thought I was losing myself in your melanin kissed skin but now I know that I am redefining myself instead. See now that I've been expose to someone who can help me heal and restore, there's nothing I wouldn't do to accomplish just that. To just be in the presence of your melanin kissed skin and your overly wise way of thinking I have grown to understand that everything happens for a reason.

Cause I'm your melanin kissed skin that I can touch with my hands and see with my dark chestnut colored eyes, I realized that regardless of if your my friend or my soulmate I'm still able to just be me and live freely and happily in knowing just that.

The Healing Process!!!

Sometimes it takes a while for a person too heal, and sometimes it does not . Personally for me I won't lie it seems like it takes an eternity for me to heal from the many hurts from life.

There are many times when I feel like I may have healed but as soon as someone try's to love me , it feels like their ripping of the scab of the unhealed wounds of my heart, mind and soul.

But to know it's all apart of the process makes me feel just a little less fearful that god is truly healing me not only on the inside but outside as well. The healing process can manifest in so many ways.

You can need healing for physical wounds or even from emotional wounds. Sometimes the wounds are socially afflicted but I find the hardest ones to overcome are those wounds that are spiritually bounded to you.

But yet in still god can heal all those wounds as well and you'll find that once the healing process begins you'll whole being will change and things that use to affect you won't anymore!

And that will be the end of your healing process because you will official be able to speak on how you have overcome all those wounds.

That will be your testimony!!! Speak life into yourself my love . Your Beautiful, your smart and your courageous and nothing will stand in your way!!!!

Losing Me!

I saw myself losing me and everything I dreamed to be. I saw myself so wrapped up in you that I cried myself to sleep. I saw myself losing every sense of direction I once had, I saw myself be lost amongst all the lies that were once said.

But now I stand here and I'm finding myself because I'm all she has left. Finding myself because I refuse to settle for less then what I'm worth . Finding myself before someone else takes a whack at my self worth, my self esteem and my confidence.

Finding myself because I know I deserve so much more than I continue to settle for but I promise I'm no longer losing myself because my baby girl is the one who needs me the most!.

Tearstained Pillowcases

Once again I'm here falling face buried in another set of tearstained pillowcases. Full of sorrows and broken hearts with nothing but nightmares and sleepless nights, with no one there to say things will be alright and that she can make it through.

The tears that stain her pillow case also cause her to have streaks upon her face. With tearstained cheeks and pillowcases she drives waway into a bottomless pit of emotion that threatens to resurface with every lump that forms in her chest. Causing the fast pace movement and fluttering of her already damaged heart.

Her tearstained pillowcases carry and guard the memories and stories of things her heart cannot begin to express. All of the agonizing pain she has endured and all the times she had to hide behind a plastered on smile,because she knew she would break if someone ever got a clear glance at her face and could tell that she had been hiding.

Days and months even years passed by she wished that the dark clouds and eyes that could not lie. That for years to come she would continue to stain her cheeks and satin pillowcases as she cried throughout the night.

the stains left on her pillowcases and the streaks of tears so wore upon her face never seem to faze anyone because she still went through life unnoticed. she was so young when the stains on her pillowcases began tears of a young child, who was lost and confused feeling betrayed and violated.

They started falling when she was only three years old, after she had been molested. Every night she would cry because she was left to believe it was her fault, then when no one was looking they would violate her again.

So on her pillowcase her tears continued to fall even when she thought her luck was changing abruptly she learned that it was only going to worsen again causing the streaks from her tears to paint lines as they dried on her cheeks.

Her eyes were made a piercing read from all the tears she had cried. See because even though she thought they was done violating her things begin to worsen, they continued even while everyone began to bully her in school.

At the end of her senior year that was full of lies because all her friends thought she wasn't a virgin anymore, although she was. They were beginning to make her wish she could die and never have to feel that pain again.

Although she didn't realize that soon enough her pillowcases would be full of teardrops again. See on one pleasant fall night her life would change drastically see remember she was a virgin, always had been although she was molested never had she been fully penetrated.

But on September 7, 2012 that would all change and the world as she knew of it would forever be altered. On that dreadful night she was violated in the worst way imaginable, losing the battle and her innocence completely.

See the teardrops were now puddles, and the pain was too much to hide, and at times too much to mask but she had to. See this once shy young lady had lost her innocence to someone she had not known, she felt like her voice was inadequate.

She fought, she screamed as his overgrown body laid upon hers as she continued to try to fight him off until so she couldn't fight any longer. She would soon return to her dorm and flood those pillowcases once again.

As she fast forwards in her story she soon realizes that she had always flooded her pillowcases. But now she would begin have thoughts of suicide and start to devise a plan she would soon attempt to see through.

Those teardrops changed to puddles that flowed and stained her pillowcases for years to come. A few years had past and after many failed attempts she was still here battered, broken and bruised but still trying to live.

Soon after her latest failed attempt to gain her wings and leave this cruel world for good. She learned that she was pregnant and that a new life was depending on her. Even through her trials she would soon give birth to her child and finish college.

Three years later and some nights she still finds herself awakened by the puddles, her eyes leave upon her satin pillowcases. As she tries to understand just why her life had turned out this way.

But she never gave up even after the tears stained her pillowcases. Her heart was broken but she kept fighting, after every loss and every letdown she stares at her child and doesn't feel so alone.

Here's to the story told from tearstained pillowcases, about how her healing would soon become all that she needed to continue to fight this ongoing battle within herself. To prove to herself and her daughter that no obstacle, trial or pain would ever stand in their way.

And there will be no more tearstained pillowcases, and red piercing eyes after crying out the last tears that her eyes could cry

Spiraling

Spiraling , falling , plunging down into a deep dark abyss with not a light in sight at the other end fighting back tears that threaten to fall from her almost to dried out eyes.

She's sinking back into a deep dark space that seems like nobody can truly ever remove her from, feeling unwanted , damaged , scarred and afraid she wanders the abyss in search of a way out.

Nobody know that's she crying out nobody gives a damn that she's smothering in her own thoughts as she continues to fight back the tears and plaster on the same smile that everyone has remembered her by.

But every night her heart and eyes singing the same tune never missing a beat but only rising an octave higher in hopes that somebody would hear , that someone would act as though they cared.

She faced with the constant battle of whether she deserves to live or if she should just end it all because not a soul would notice , yeah you're thinking life cant possible be that hard for her and she's most likely being over dramatic.

But see everyday she goes to war although it feels like it's endless, she try's to fight and remain strong but she too just wants someone to cherish her, value her and hold her and let her know she's not alone and she is loved.

But instead she's giving the cold shoulder by most and ignored by all of those she's always been there for , her tears flow like endless streams and oceans , the current is so strong it threatens the very exists of all things living and non living.

She's just longing for a way out, a friend but is only faced with more letdowns and is on the verge of a complete shutdown she wants to end it all but as she looks into what seems to be a mirror displaying the most accurate image of a child who looks exactly like her she realizes that this fight is never going to be over.

Cause she's trying to heal from all things that she never speaks of and no one even knows that it's killing her inside and all she wants is love so that the tears stop falling and she can place her feet firmly back on solid ground.

Spinning, spiraling, and twisting about in the cold cruel world that doesn't give a damn about anyone else except itself. Fearing failure but struggling and wrestling to find the drive to fight, to try, to simply just live and succeed.

She lays awake at night drowning in the ever flowing puddles and seas of emotions, thoughts, dreams and insecurities hoping to find one person who will vow to always help her stay afloat.

Inner Beauty

how do I start to figure out
   how beautiful I really am
   inside and out but honestly
   the only beauty that matters
   is my inner beauty.
   No matter who or what is said
   I know that I'm beautiful.
   I try hard to cover it up
   but it never seems to go as planned,
   because my inner beauty can't be lost
   that's my self-confidence.
   Nobody can rid you of your beauty
   all they can do is make you question it.
   so many times I have felt as though
   I wasn't beautiful, but now I know
   I will always be beautiful
   inside and out.
   Inner beauty can not be taking away
   altered or changed.
   everything you go through
   helps that inner beauty to grow
   and helps to create a wall
   that can't be torn down
   that's my self-worth.
   So with that combination of
   self-worth, self-confidence and
   inner beauty.
   what someone else thinks
   should never matter to you.
   you're perfect just the way you are

on the inside and out.
That's true inner beauty
what everyone else envies.

Triggers

My therapist once told me I should try to identify my triggers, she once told me these triggers could be people, places or things. But what she didn't tell me was these triggers could just be seasons, songs or even mentions of certain words that can begin to cause that heart wrenching feeling you get during a panic attack or simply just being put in situations that resemble those things.

Oh no she never said I could look at someone who's characteristic remind me of my mom and instantly started to feel those years of being silenced, blamed and abused come rushing back to me full speed ahead without warning. But hey she did say try to identify my biggest triggers and even put a name to them.

So hey mom it hurts to say that your trigger number one because even know as an adult, I'm still longing and craving to hear you say I'm proud of you and I love you. But all that plays in my head like a broken disc in a Walkmen you bought from me that my cousin dropped and now it doesn't work is you could've done better or I'm just so disappointed.

Hey mom I know when you look at me you say hey there's the child who's taken on so many things but still won't try her best. But hey mom I also know when you look at me it's like you're starring at yourself in a mirror your mini version of you with all the trauma and generational curses and yet and still I just want to feel loved and appreciated by you.

And then there's dad, hey pops I miss you and even more I miss how close we once were, cause sadly know I can't even muscle up the strength or mental energy to come see you anymore. And no dad it's not your fault completely but the little girl in me has always just wanted her dad to be her "dad".

Instead this little girl manage to create a void and then fill it just to find out there was never truly a void. I'll always be daddy's little girl, the one who made you a father and the one who made you a grandfather. But all I long for is just some daddy daughter time nothing more. I want you to know I'm no longer angry I just want you to fill the space of that void.

And now I move on to someone I never identified as one of my triggers but god knows she probably takes the cake. Hello to my dad's wife I don't know you anymore. Behind the alcohol and the cigarette mask a person who has let life take her and spit her out, so cruel so ornery but yet I'm told I still have to respect her.

I'm not a little kid anymore respected is earned not given and I'm for damn sure not respecting a soul that doesn't respect me or my boundaries anymore so away I went and you still don't get it I loved you like no other. My bonus mom never once allowed anyone to disrespect that was until you showed me known.

But enough about you hello abandonment issues yeah I'm calling you out, you have made me believe for years that nobody could ever love or want me around. But today I'm here to tell you that's a lie no doubt see everyday there are people who fight to show me otherwise. And no I don't always believe their words but their actions always seem to stand out.

See since I child I was afraid that everyone would always leave me by myself but then God sent an angel and his name is Shawndel. See Shawndel came around when I literally had no one and from day one he's shown me that he's around for the ride and that's no cap. He saw me when no one else did or could, shit he's loved me through it all. Shawndel that my rider and he's never needed no help.

So abandonment issues you can't reside here no more cause after Shawndel came around and stuck around for more than a year I learned that my issue with you steamed from a mother and a father who have felt that way themselves. I'm thankful for the few friends I have because they've been with me for years shit some of them even witness the birth of my kid.

So I say so long to you and hello to fear. Fear of rejection and never being enough. But most importantly fear of myself. Yes I said fear of myself because I know I could be doing so much more. But I've taken on the imposter syndrome and I don't apply myself anymore, cause in the back of my mind I'm always thinking to myself what's the point anymore.

So that fear lead me to some people that I leave nameless, they're nameless because I gave them way to much value when they couldn't even manage to respect my boundaries. They've slandered my name and went against the grain, they know I would've laid my life down and died from them but now they not have not a single name.

So as we travel down more we say hello to generational curses and being the black sheep. See I never signed up for either one of these but yet I am that black sheep and I was positioned and called to break these generational curses that I wasn't even around to see be built brick by brick so damn high I don't even talk to my family much none of them on either side.

I've always longed for a close relationship with them but see I've learned over the years that's not what they want in return. So here I lay it all to rest I'll stay around the ones who love me for me and push me to do great things, cause believe it or not without me these generational curses will remain a thing. But I say no way it stops with me.

Now I say hello to depression and anxiety. Depression, anxiety and me have a love hate relationship where they love me but I hate them. Because these to leave me feeling low and stagnant just afraid to truly love me and to succeed. They threatened to ruin every relationship I constantly fought for and mad me feel like I wasn't worthy of anything.

But today I say depression and anxiety they have to loosen they're hold but cause I have things to accomplish and dreams to live. I'm done fighting with the suicidal thoughts and the lack of self worth they bring to me. I know I deserve to be here to be alive to be happy and that's all I'm striving for.

Now as I continued down this road I need now to put fake friendships on blast because for too long I've made myself believe that I am a terrible friend. That I don't show up or love my friends out loud.

But she that's not true where they say I don't always show up I show up in the capacity that I can show up. Loving them from my love language because I'm unsure of theirs.

See I've lost some friends I thought I would never lose, learned some things about those I would constantly defend to my family. Just for them to turn their backs on me and try to make me out to be the bad guy, but sadly for them I no longer force them to stay around or defend myself against the narratives they try to spin about me.

Finally I need to speak to the little girl in me because although she's not a trigger per say, I need her to know that she is worthy and she is loved. She's valued, appreciated and wanted never should she feel otherwise. So dear little me I love you and I'm sorry that we tend to trigger each other which sends our minds wondering in the abyss questioning our very existence but no more I say. No more

A Person Lost

I dream about you morning, noon and night thinking about how everything in the multi universe seems to end the instant ours worlds collided. There was this intense magnetic pull that gravitated our energies as one.

One song, one heart, one last chance on love and it caused my heart to skip three more beats and left me senseless and unable to communicate the feelings I would soon begin to radiate out into the deepest parts of your hemispheres.

One song that was stuck on an infinite loop replaying the exact time and day we met , with just a few stolen glances and an exchange of hellos I was stuck to you like flames to a tree, setting ablaze all the doubts I had in my mind on love.

One heart constantly dancing amongst the daisy in a field that's endless and full of love, peace and serenity. The way our hearts intertwined with one another it was like the ancestors knew we would attract each other, and all while healing, building and loving each other unconditionally.

Would it sound completely off the wall if I said I wasn't looking for this man, but he swooped in with the right healing and loving powers that I need. Godsend is what he is and I love this for me a sense of home is felt in him. He's my person.

Yes, I said he's my PERSON what can I say everything about that man from his walk, to his talk, from the way his words caress my ears when he jokes around with me. Even the way his fingers gentle caress my body then find a way to intertwine between mine. Leaving me starstruck and in a daze. I'm at home!

That man with his beautifully sun kissed skin of melanin to his dark colored chestnut eyes, that bore into my soul unleashing every secret and desire I have. The one who feeds my soul and boost my self esteem I love this man for me. I pray that he will one day feel all these things about me.

One song, one heart, one soul equally yoked and steadfast in the lord. He loves me through and past my mess while I graciously do the same to him. He took me from being so masculine to living within my soft feminine energy without a care in the world. Two hearts coming together as one.

The time has come to separate and part but not forever just for now as we collectively and separately continue to grow. The love we share running deeper than either one of us could imagine. But what is for us will always be given to us. So will we may have to part ways for a while. We both know that the love we have will not.

Just Being Me!

I heard I made you happy today,
    But see today I am very proud,
    See all I ever wanted was to see
    You smile and to make you happy,
    Maybe even proud.
    Even though my words aren't verbal,
    They are still being heard,
    All my dopiest rhymes,
    All my inner thoughts being
    Expressed for the first time all,
    Written down on paper for
    The world to see.
    See me I am young,
    Shy and always ready
    To give up completely,
    But I continue to fit
    No matter how hard it gets.
    I remember when I was always,
    Concerned about what others thought,
    And what they would say, see all
    That doesn't matter, it's not
    Important anymore what others
    Think and say about me.
    I'm shinning bright today,
    Through every rhyme and
    Every pain I learned that,
    My voice too deserves to
    Be heard and it will be
    Heard, yes loud and clear.
    As I scream everything that

makes me, ME, I begin to
heal from the inside out.
Through the pain, through
the tears even through
every contagious laugh.
Hey, see this right here,
This here is my thing. Sometimes
I slip up and glance down
at the floor.
As shy as I was, and
sometimes I can't help but
to glance down at the floor,
but this isn't where I got my
chance, but I look them straight
in the face, laugh and smile,
cause see I had the last laugh,
the last words this time.

Scattered Dreams

These are the words I've always wanted to say: the memories of a girl with shattered dreams, Dreams that she wishes she could just pick up and glue back together but the pieces just don't seem to fit.

The dreams of a girl who had extremely high hopes for herself that went on a path to self-destruction. A girl who just wanted to be loved unconditionally by those whom she showed her love too unconditionally. Her shattered dreams became haunting realities when she took the wrong path looking for love in all the wrong places.

It all began September 7 2012, one cool fall night in Buffalo where she thought she was safe to walk around her complex talking on the phone, not knowing she would eventually meet the guy that would change her life and her views on love completely. She didn't know that would be the night she would lose her innocence completely along with her self-worth.

That night indeed changed her life forever, she was never the same person. The young girl who had such high hopes, she was gonna be a pediatrician.

Now she would have to uproot her life one more time to start all over again because she was running away from the one person who said he wouldn't hurt her. Dreams shattered by the events playing over and over in her head, of being raped by a complete stranger.

But that was only the beginning of her dreams starting to shattered, she soon would lose grandmother after grandmother of whom she was close to aunts and uncles and even cousin seemed like life was just out to shatter her hope.

But she continued to push she enrolled in school and changed her career path, but that was only the beginning for more setbacks. Her biggest one yet to come, would be her falling for a guy who promised her a life to together and a family. Never ending solid dreams becoming shattered realities and there was nothing she could do about it.

Those lies turned to realities when she found out she was pregnant and without hesitation he was gone, never to return, never to be there. The story doesn't stop there, it continues, where she thinks she finds a light, someone is there trying to shatter the rest of those dreams she has dreamed.

Will the girl allow all her dreams to be shattered or will she get up and fight? Only time will tell and she won't be the one who tells it her child will!

Internal Happiness

We all are longing for a sense of happiness that is unwavering and untouchable. You know that internal happiness you get from a day of protect your energy and staying out of rooms you have already outgrew.

We search our whole lives to find it but sadly some never do, that's why I've dedicated my time to healing so in return I can receive just that you know.

Some will say I'll never reach or I'll never find it , forever damaged and brokenhearted I'll forever remain. But I fight with my fist tightly clenched until I do exactly what my heart desires and that to find that internal happiness that money can't buy me and no one else can give me.

See I find part of my internal happiness when I was blessed with the gift of being my daughter into this uncertain world, and with every passing day she has shown me that all the happiness I need is right within my reach.

Safe Place

You've always been my safe place away from the noise, the person I can trust with ever fiber of my being to love and value me and to create a space where I feel safe. Over the years we've invested I've grown even more fonder of you and the memories we share.

But as time progresses I've come to realize you became my safe place that barricaded me from so many storms all in all while causing many other lil storms to arise within me. My safe place away from the aches and pains from the things I feel I could never explain.

My safe place when the world seems to always be so gray, the place I go when nobody understands the mannerisms that makeup the fibers of my being. My escape-goat into a world that is not my reality. A false reality you have presented to me.

It has been a while since we've last talked but I just want you to know forever you will be my safe place but I'm just not in love with you anymore. Safe is how I feel with you and that will never change but this time around I'll leave my feelings out of it so our friendship never changes.

My safe place you'll always remain!

Cold Hearted

There was a time when I used to let my heart lead but in return I was always left bleeding so now that I'm turning cold now the world just wanna know where did the old me go. That girl has died with the last piece of humanity because you only love someone when you can't no longer have them.

Just let me be, just let me breathe. I am suffocating in a world that can only decipher things through rose colored lenses and it just ain't for me. Too many times I've given second chances to so many motherfuckers who never could or would do the same for me.

I guess yall don't hear me when I said the storm in me was getting ready to blow upstream and wipe out everything you thought we could be. Baby please don't cry for me cause when you had me it wasn't enough so you made it seem.

Stop wasting my time if you don't really accept me please I'm begging you just leave me the fuck be. I don't have any space in my world for the uncertainty you play with me cause you are faced with demons in your dreams.

You lay with me cause I usually don't say a thing but here I am screaming now please just leave me tf be but still you try to make me seem like I'm the problem when in all actuality baby it's you can't you see. You won't face your truth and just be you play charades everyday say it ain't the truth.

Now you're saying I'm a cold hearted bitch and baby just maybe I might be what looks at everything y'all put me through but nobody else would blame me for the cold hearted truth that bleeds onto this page not an ending in sight shit I'm just getting started to tell you the truth.

You be screaming be my fucking peace and baby to tell you the truth when you come around it's nothing but pain and strife. You serve confusion and chaos on a platter with one side of grief. Because I'm grieving what could've been but faced with the harsh reality of why will never be.

But trust me baby, the love isn't lost, you just can't ever reside here anymore because I'm more concerned about myself and my growth and all you were giving me was pain and broken promises. And now baby I'm cold.

Yearning For Love

I'm yearning for a love so pure that kinda love you see on the screens of every electronic device in your reach. The kinda love that papa and nana had back in the day, that unwavering love, that unexplainable unconditional compromising love.

I want a love that will linger on with me even after we have withered away with age. Because that love could never be severed with ascending age, with every strand of hair that goes from a specific shade of one color on the color wheel to gray, with every valley and through every peak we rise like a skyscraper from the ground.

The kind of love that can move mountains no matter the weather we are faced with. The love that sets the tone for the generations that follow in our footsteps. An unshakable love that can stand the test of time. A solid foundation equally yoked that the Lord God himself sent to us to be unmovable.

An explanation of what perfection could be even though the mere thought of being perfect is unattainable. A steady love like the love that is hummed in almost every song I hear on the radio. I love that I can love me even at my worst and most certainly at my best.

Our love is like my favorite love song, replaying a thousand and one times in my head with a steady tempo and heartfelt lyrics. A love that wakes me up with a smile and allows me to sleep peacefully at night. That golden love, that steadfast love. A love that's not black and white.

But a love so pure we can discover the rarest shades of every color there has ever been known to man. You see I'm yearning for a love that will be sent to me. A love that would have me hunched over in tears cause I'm your wife to be.

Enough

In the stillness of the night we lay in our dwelling place plagued by the demon of uncertainty and overthinking. See uncertainty comes with no boundaries and as for overthinking well you get right. The misconception that you'll never be enough, have enough you're just simply not enough.

In due time they say you'll heal and those two who have come unannounced, uninvited and ever so intrusive in your heart, your mind and soul must pack their bags cause they cannot dwell here anymore. You look at yourself, tears caressing your checks and begin to think.

Hey you , yes you the one listening, the one observing, the one crying , the one who's simply just trying to get by. You hear in the stillness of the room through the silence that fills the room with gloom and sorrow that there's no hope left here for you.

Overtaken by sadness and loneliness you scour around frantically looking for just a morsel of strength to keep on going, you soon realize that as the days go by it gets hard to do so. You soon realize that anxiety and depression have come in to run amuck.

With no warning and absolutely manual on how to navigate through the treacherous waters you are stuck at a standstill questioning your own existence while placing everyone else's burden upon yourself. You forget that you deserve to feel loved, seen and wanted.

As the days go by you begin to feel alone and caged in by the thoughts of never being deserving or loved till one day it hits you like a ton of bricks that you indeed deserve to be loved and cared for and that the right person will come along and change your mind and calm your heart.

Seeing that piece I was missing before is no longer lost. I've prayed about this for entirely way too long and I know that it's for me because of the way we both try to pour into each other nothing that is short of love. Without saying those three words I know in my heart I am more than enough and now my heart is full.

Because you simply make me feel like I am way more than just ENOUGH!

Growth

In these quiet moments of reflection, I find myself longing for personal growth. To shed the shell of who I once was, And emerge as a stronger, wiser soul.

Like a seed planted in fertile soil, I seek nourishment for my spirit to thrive. Through challenges and triumphs alike, I push myself to reach for new heights.

Each trial a lesson, each success a milestone, I am constantly evolving, ever-changing. My mind expands, my heart opens, As I embrace the journey of self-discovery.

It is in the struggle that I find my strength, In the darkness that I discover my light. I am a work in progress, a masterpiece in the making, Unveiling layers of myself with each passing day.

I welcome growth with open arms, Embracing the unknown with courage and grace. For I am a gardener of my own soul, Cultivating a life rich with depth and meaning.

So here I stand, a testament to resilience, A beacon of hope for those who seek their own path. Personal growth is not a destination, but a journey, And I am grateful for every step along the way.

This journey that I've embarked on to rediscover my true self, hasn't always been easy but indeed I've grown. Into myself, into my true essence with a little bit of faith the size of a mustard seed and hope for things that are still unknown.

Out of my comfort zone I sprout, just like the seeds that are planted into the ground. Stronger, wiser and even more beautiful because every obstacle and trial I've embraced with a little more grace and resilience as the days go on.

This is my journey and I know it's never complete because with each passing day I continue to grow and evolve into who I always dreamed I would become.

Forever Evolving

Upon the canvas of our lives we paint,
A masterpiece, evolving without restraint,
From the depths of our souls, we rise,
To reach new heights, beyond the skies.

With every dawn, a chance to grow,
To shed old skin, and let new chapters flow,
In the journey of self-evolution,
We find our truest resolution.

Like a mighty oak, we stand tall,
Roots running deep, never to fall,
Through storms and trials, we endure,
Becoming stronger, more mature.

With each passing year, we learn,
From every joy, and every burn,
We shape ourselves, in ways unseen,
Becoming who we're meant to be.

The caterpillar sheds its cocoon,
Emerging as a butterfly, too soon,
A symbol of transformation,
A testament to our dedication.

We shed our doubts, our fears, our pain,
    And in its place, we plant the seed of gain,
    For in the soil of our souls,
    We find the strength to make us whole.

Through self-reflection, we discover,
    The power within, like no other,
    To shape our destiny, to mold our fate,
    To walk the path, we create.

So let us embrace this journey,
    With open hearts, and minds that yearn,
    For in the process of self-evolution,
    We find the essence of our true solution.

Dear Little Me

In the depths of my heart, there's a place just for you
A time in my life that's forever true
So many memories of when I was young
And now I look back and see all that I've become

Dear little me, I write to you today
    To share with you the wisdom I've gained along the way
    You were innocent and full of bliss
    But life is not always as simple as this

I remember the days of running free
    Of laughing and playing, climbing trees
    But I also recall the moments of pain
    The tears that fell like a never-ending rain

I want to tell you, little one, to hold on tight
    To cherish every moment, every day and night
    Because life will throw you curveballs that you won't expect
    But with determination and courage, you'll always deflect

You see, little me, you're stronger than you know
    You'll face battles and struggles, but you'll always grow
    Don't be afraid to speak up and stand your ground
    Your voice matters, it's important, let it resound

Don't let anyone dim your light, little me
    You're a shining star, you're meant to be
    There will be times when you feel lost and alone
    But remember, you're never truly on your own

I wish I could shield you from all the pain
    From the heartbreak and loss that will leave a stain
    But know that every trial will shape you into who you are
    You'll rise from the ashes, you'll reach for the stars

Embrace your uniqueness, your quirks and flaws
    They make you special, they're your own applause
    Don't compare yourself to others, don't strive to fit in
    Be proud of who you are, let your journey begin

Take risks, little me, don't be afraid to fail
    It's in those moments that you'll set sail
    On a path of discovery, of growth and change
    You'll learn to embrace the unfamiliar and the strange

Hold onto your dreams, let them guide your way
    They'll lead you to joy and fulfillment each day
    Don't let fear hold you back, spread your wings and fly
    You're capable of greatness, reach for the sky

And most importantly, little me, remember to love

UNAPOLOGETIC BLUE BUTTERFLY

    To love yourself deeply, with all that you're made of
    You deserve happiness, you deserve peace
    You deserve a life filled with love, never cease

So here's my letter to you, dear little me
    To remind you of all that you can be
    I hope you'll look back and see how far you've come
    And know that with love and courage, you'll always overcome.

Healing From My Trauma

In the shadows of the past,
Lies a pain that never fades,
A trauma that holds us fast,
In its dark and tangled maze.
But healing is a journey,
That we must all embark upon,
To find peace and sanctuary,
In the light of a new dawn.
It starts with facing the pain,
And acknowledging its grip,
Not trying to contain,
The emotions that often slip.
It's okay to feel afraid,
To feel anger, sadness, and grief,
But in time, those feelings fade,
And we find some relief.
Therapy can be a lifeline,
A safe space to work through,
The trauma that confines,
And shapes everything we do.
Talking through our fears,
And learning coping strategies,
Helps to dry our tears,
And release the pain that besieges.
Self-care is essential,
To healing from trauma's hold,
Taking care of our mental,
And physical well-being, bold.
Meditation and mindfulness,
Can help calm a troubled mind,

UNAPOLOGETIC BLUE BUTTERFLY

Connecting to our inner bliss,
And leaving the past behind.
Exercise and healthy eating,
Nourish our bodies and souls,
Creating a strong beating,
Heart that helps make us whole.
Finding support in loved ones,
And building a community,
Of understanding and compassion,
Can be a key to unity.
Art and creativity,
Can also be a healing balm,
Expressing our emotions freely,
Through writing, painting, or a calming psalm.
Nature's healing power,
Can also soothe our aching souls,
Walking through a quiet bower,
Or admiring beauty that consoles.
Healing from trauma takes time,
And patience with ourselves,
It's a mountain we must climb,
With gentle steps and inner wells.
But know that there is hope,
In every sunrise that we see,
For healing is a way to cope,
And set our wounded spirits free.
So take each moment as it comes,
And know that you are not alone,
In the journey to healing from,
The trauma that once overthrown.
With courage and resilience,
And love from those who care,

We can find our inner brilliance,
And rise above despair.
Healing from trauma is possible,
And though the road is long,
With support, love, and a will,
We can emerge more strong.

About the Author

CeeCee The Butterfly a single mom of one who is embracing herself and embarking on a self-exploration and self healing journey through poetry. She uses poetry as a way to slow readers to get to know her in her most vulnerable state while encouraging and fostering the readers own journey to healing.